Positive Thinking

Learn to Have an Optimistic Outlook for a Happier More Successful Life (Destroy Stress and Self-Doubt)

C.A. Barry

Introduction

When you learn to get your brain on your side, life seems to get easier. Our happiness, ability to achieve success and solve problems in our lives, all revolve around how we use what we have. The best poker players in the world can be dealt a terrible hand of cards and yet still flip it, so they win the round. This book is a guide to start training you to view the world in a whole different light. You can change the way your brain functions, so it works in the most beneficial way possible for you. You can get the health, wealth and happiness you want by learning how to get your brain on your side.

This book will teach you the following:

- How to master your mind, so it works for you.
- The most empowering belief you can develop.
- How to deal with failures and use them to propel you forward.
- How to access your true creative potential.
- The missing key to learning any skill and achieving the success you want.
- ...and much more.

The earlier you change the way your brain works, the earlier you'll get the results you want in life. Thank you for buying this book and enjoy.

Table of Contents

The Greatest Obstacle You Will Ever Need To Overcome

When you change the way you perceive events, the events themselves consequently change. So much of our idea of reality is based on what our mind chooses to focus on. Our brain creates filters for information that we are barely even aware of. It's of an extreme advantage to be able to help choose and guide these filters to suit our best interests.

If you want evidence of this, you can merely search Daniel Simmons' world famous awareness test. In the test, you are asked to count how many times the team in white pass the basketball. So at the end of the test you catch yourself saying "Oh that was easy," in glory of your accomplishment. It then, however, takes an unexpected turn and asks you if you noticed the gorilla in the middle of it. If you rewind the video and watch it again, there is quite clearly a man dressed as a gorilla who walked in, very unsubtly and beat his chest and then walked out. The majority of people never even knew he was there. Imagine you had this type of blind spot towards success. Opportunities may have presented themselves and because of the way you perceive the world, you might not have even seen or noticed them. This is what happens all the time to your standard negative thinker, because they view the world in a negative light. Positive opportunities and events could present themselves, but they barely even get recognised because of this.

To illustrate this idea further, let's discuss the story of a person named "S. B. Fuller". Mr. Fuller belonged to a family of Negro farmers in the state of Louisiana. He began working when he was just five years old. This situation was prevalent among tenant farmers. His family was so poor that Samuel was forced to drop out of school at sixth grade to help out his family. Samuel's mother instilled the idea to him that you do not always have to be poor, that it was possible to change your circumstances. An idea can be infectious; it can take over your entire mind and change the world around you. In the words of Leonardo Di Caprio in the movie Inception, "A single idea from the human mind can build cities. An idea can transform the world and rewrite all the rules." This is what happened to Samuel, he was determined to change his circumstances and whole-heartedly believed it could be done.

He sold soaps for twelve years. He learned the importance of patience, hard work, and positive thoughts. He then went on to purchase the company who produced the soaps he was selling and founded Fuller Products. He became so successful that he was able to purchase seven more businesses.

It's important to point out that most people had more advantages than what Mr. Fuller had. However, he had a grand goal and did all that he can could to reach it. Obviously, establishing goals is a personal thing. You will set your goals based on your preferred criteria. Some people don't want to manage large corporations. Some individuals don't want to be great actors or painters. Goals differ from person to person.

Regardless of your goals, you can be the person you want to be using your mind to help attract the things you want in the world and to view your reality in the most beneficial way for you.

To attain greatness, it is a massive advantage to be passionate about what you are working on. Steve Jobs gave a rather famous interview alongside Bill Gates at the D5 conference in 2007. He stated that often the difference between people who are successful in society is that the people who succeed love what they do. As he explains about the people that make it, "Often times it's the ones who love what they do, so they could persevere when it got really tough. And the ones that didn't love it, quit. Because they're sane, right? Who would put up with this stuff if you don't love it?" Love for what you do will help drive you through the tough times when others give up.

Two Important Lessons

Henry J. Kaiser was considered the father of modern American shipbuilding and founder of Kaiser Family Foundation, which is a non-profit charity. He learned two important lessons that led him to great success from his mother (Mary Kaiser). These lessons helped create the core beliefs that helped him rise to the success he was. These lessons are:

- You can get the things you want in life if you are willing to work for them and put in the effort. If you are willing to work, and you change the way you view work; you can then learn to enjoy it. Mr. Kaiser considered this "joy" as a priceless gift. When you enjoy the process, you've already won, and the results will start to fall into place as an added bonus.

- Giving and loving people are two of the most satisfying things you can do.

The Continuous Battle Between Positivity And Negativity

By thinking positively, you can attract the things you want to have in life. Negative thinking, however, can sap your energy and make your life an endless nightmare.

Positive thinking involves the following words (and the characteristics they represent): hope, courage, tact, optimism, faith, tolerance, integrity, kindness, generosity and common sense. A person who has Positive thinking establishes high objectives and does everything in his power to achieve them and then some.

Negative thinking is the exact opposite of Positive thinking.

Your Greatest Obstacle

Think of all your greatest naysayers. All the people who drag you down and sap your belief that you can do the things you want. The obstacles stopping you getting where you want to be. It's sad to say, but you're probably thinking of family and close friends. There was a woman called Lisa on a date, she was all dressed up and already sitting at the table waiting for her date. The Lisa's phone vibrates. She looks at the message and sees that her date has cancelled on her. She phones up her friend and her friend then comes down to meet and comfort her. When Lisa meets her friend and begins to explain, her friend replies "It's because you are too fat, and your hair, it just isn't nice." The woman takes this very badly. This is not a very good friend to have. Only Lisa never rang her friend, the person who said those things was Lisa. It was her thoughts that were saying these things, at a time when she needed comforting. If it is another person, you would be baffled, but when it's ourselves talking, we seem to have no problem accepting it. The story is from a psychologist called Guy Winch and tries to show the reader how hard we can be on ourselves at times where we need comforting. Other people aren't your greatest obstacle, you are. The only way people from the outside can get to you is if you allow them to. You are the most influential person in your life.

The moment you use positive thinking, you will meet the most important person in your life. Well, YOU are that important person (as far as your life and future are concerned). The remaining chapters of this book will provide you with different principles related to positive thinking. By mastering these principles, your mind will be more powerful. Consequently, you will drastically increase your chances of success towards your goals in life (e.g. wealth, health, success, happiness, etc.).

The Surprisingly Most Empowering Belief You Can Have

Most people have experienced a hard failure at some point in their lives. If you haven't, then you really haven't tried to achieve anything of significant value, as true triumphs have to be earned. When faced with failure the modern day answer to it seems to be excuses. There are such a wide variety of excuses the modern-day human being could use. Everything from, I grew up in a bad household to the person performing the interview was someone who just didn't like me. I am going to introduce you to a very harsh and a very extreme way of thinking. Although it is harsh, it is empowering. If a problem or situation has you in it, it's your fault. If you think like this, you will be able to do things other people couldn't dream of because you think differently than they do.

If you think this way and do not give yourself the satisfaction of having any excuses for anything, success will just come as a by-product. If anything has you in the equation, take full unflinching responsibility for it. Guess what, if it is your fault, that means you have the power to change it. For example if you fail at a job interview, it is your fault. If before that interview you had worked on yourself, went to extra conferences, extra seminars, read extra books and truly maximised your skills to the full potential, would you have got the job? It is not the responsibility of people taking the job interviews to get you a job. It is their responsibility to get the person who will be the most useful to them. If you had studied far beyond the means that would be expected for that job, and if you had gone above and beyond, and it's between you and one other person. They might like the other person far more, but if you were going to earn the company an extra $50,000 a year, then 99% of the time, they'll go with you. If you look back on your life, think of all the things you could have done if you had this mindset. Another example would be; if you're an athlete and you start playing bad, and let your opponents or the crowd get to you. Take responsibility for it. It is your responsibility to become more mentally resilient. If you don't know how, look up books on it and read them or simply Google it. In an ideal world, that obstacle wouldn't be there, but this is not an ideal world, so it's up to you.

It seems to be a common phenomenon for people to believe they were not born with the talent it takes to do great things. It is our responsibility to do the best with what we've got. I'm not a religious person, I'm more scientifically minded but a lot of the time people blame God for their situation and hope that God chooses them to win the lottery or some divine intervention to change their life. When I was younger my family was religious, so I went to church. I remember a particular story one of the priests told which go like this; There was a great storm predicted to come into town, and the people were told to evacuate. There was a man who we'll call Tom. The Neighbours called at his door and said: "Tom we need to get out of here, the storm is coming." Tom replied, "No I won't God will save me." A couple of hours pass and the town begins to flood. The townspeople call at Tom's door, this time, they're in a boat due to the flood. They shout, "Tom you need to come with us now, we might not be able to get to you later!" Tom replied, "No, God will save me." A few more hours pass and the water level gets so high, it floods the house and Tom's sitting on the roof. People come in a helicopter this time and say "Tom you need to come now, you are going to die!" Once again Tom says "No, God will save me." Eventually, Tom dies, and he goes to heaven and confronts God. He asks: "God why didn't you save me?" God replies, "I sent you a car, a boat, and a helicopter, what more do you want?" Basically, the point of the story is, don't wait for miracles to happen, do everything in your power to make them happen.

Here's an important idea that you should remember: if you

want to change your world, you need to begin with yourself. Once you become your "best self," your world will also be in its best form. This is the core idea behind Positive thinking. If you have a positive attitude, you can beat your problems, or you can change the way you view them.

You Were Born to Succeed

Genetically there is no one like you. You are unique, even if you have a twin brother/sister, your fingerprints, and the way your brain develops is different. No one in the world was born like you. Additionally, nobody will be born like you ever again. You are a collection of atoms formed in a particularly unique way that will never be replicated. I do not believe there are ever dreams given to us that we weren't supposed to fulfil. I believe they are our souls call to action, and if we don't at least try for them we spend the rest of our lives dealing with the pain of "What if". I believe there's a reason we are always the star of our own dreams; I believe it's our subconscious telling us to go and reach for these greater things.

The Specifics of your Objectives

Positive thinking and having specific objectives serve as the beginning of any significant success. Remember that the world changes every day, even if you want things to stay as they are. You can help guide these changes and change their general direction. You may choose your objectives. After identifying your goals, go after them. Try developing yourself in the following areas to maximise your probability of success.

1. Enthusiasm
2. Organized thinking
3. Creativity
4. Initiative
5. Attention
6. Self-discipline
7. Ability to budget resources (i.e. money and time)

According to a recent study, 98% of people who are not contented with their "current universe" don't know the kind of universe they want to be in. This fact is completely staggering. It means that many people live their life aimlessly, discontented, fighting countless things but without any specific goal. At this point, can you enumerate your goals in life? Establishing "fixed goals" can be hard. It may actually involve long, painful self-examinations. This exercise is worthwhile, however, regardless of the costs it involves. As soon as you establish a specific goal, you will enjoy the following benefits:

1. Your mind will work according to a universal principle: "If you can think about it and believe in it, you can achieve it." Since you are visualizing your goal, your mind will function based on your own suggestions. As a result, your mind will help you reach your destinations.

2. Since you are aware of your goal, you'll be able to find the right path and go in the right direction. You will be action-oriented.

3. If you use positive thinking, you can. You can learn how to enjoy your tasks. You will be motivated to do the important stuff. Your enthusiasm will improve as you visualize your goals more. Since you are enthusiastic, desire becomes your burning passion.

4. You can identify opportunities as soon as they present themselves. You know what you want to get, so your senses are more attuned to finding opportunities related to your goals.

Positive Thinking Exercise

Look back to a lot of the events that had you personally involved in them and that didn't go as well as you had hoped. Now I want you to accept total responsibility for them. Even if the issue was only 1% your fault, think of how you could have done even a fraction better. Think of what ways you could have done more and changed the odds to more in your favour. I know what you're thinking, "A book on positivity getting me to do this, what is that about?" However you have to trust me, you see as soon as you accept responsibility for it, you empower yourself. You view the Universe in a different way. You don't view as something doing upon on to you, but something you have the power to change. Don't beat yourself up for these failures, just accept responsibility, learn what you would do better the next time and move on.

-

Your Emotions Are Not On Your Side

A human's mind contains certain thoughts and ideas that act as "cobwebs" that affect the processes inside it. Even the brightest minds suffer from it. Negative habits, passions, feelings, beliefs, and emotions act as cobwebs that ruin the speed and clarity of your thought processes. Think of all the times something bad has happened which then causes you to relive it over and over in your head. It is no use reliving the past event in your head if you can no longer do anything about it. Yet we do this, and it inhibits our ability to get back in that working headspace. Emotional intelligence is of extreme importance when it comes to success; so being able to flip a situation around and think positively is an extremely useful skill. When you catch yourself in one of these situations, try to break the thought loop. Set a timer for 3 minutes and force yourself to think of anything else, think of something mundane. Focus on it no matter what and be strict about it. Even doing this for 2 minutes will help break the thought loops, so you can get back to work.

In some cases, you have bad habits that you need to correct. Some situations, lure you in with instant gratification, instant payoffs but taking the easy way out becomes like a fly that got trapped in the web of a spider, and you experience problems freeing yourself. Your "actual" will collides with your primal instincts to get instant payoffs, instant reliefs or smaller victory. Our emotions and instincts a lot of the time are not on our side. Many individuals surrender and suffer from mental clashes. Some people, on the other hand, discover how to use their conscious will to access their subconscious one. This is an extremely useful weapon in your arsenal. Succeeding through Positive Thinking will teach you how to utilize your conscious and subconscious powers.

You're just a human being. You will surely get caught in these metaphorical spider webs inside your head. Whenever you get caught, you will have problems liberating yourself; it will be tuff. However, you have one thing that you can control completely, your mental attitude. You may clear away your mental cobwebs. You destroy these "webs" before they even form. With Positive thinking, you can learn to tackle any obstacle.

You can use "thinking prowess" and positive thinking to maintain clarity in your mind.

There was an experiment conducted on children at Stanford University. The title of the experiment was dubbed as "The Marshmallow Experiment" and went along these lines; The children were presented with one marshmallow placed in front of them. They were then told they could either eat the one marshmallow now or they could wait, and the person conducting the test would give them two. The children were then left alone for a time period with their marshmallow. Some children ate the one marshmallow while others managed to last the 15 or so minutes and got their reward. The interesting thing, however, is when they followed up on the children years later. The children who were able to hold off the instant gratification for the reward of two marshmallows showed a direct correlation to higher test scores. Due to the ability of being able to put an instant reward away in order to achieve a better reward was a quality suggested by the results which allowed them to suffer momentary "pain" in this case studying for a higher end goal which in this case was achieving better grades. It's of extreme importance to be able to delay gratification to achieve the success that you strive for. It is a mental skill that you can develop.

Positivity Exercise-Meditation

Learning how to meditate can train you to, not let your emotions get in the way of clear judgement. It also is one of the only proven methods that makes you happier. If you haven't tried it, it's most definitely worth a go. It also improves higher brain function and will power, as it develops your prefrontal cortex in your brain which is basically the part of the brain where your will power comes from. If you are not sure how to do it, I have a book on happiness which goes pretty in depth on it and I'll write the name at the end or you can simply search for other books on it. It is a powerful tool.

Exploring your Mind's True Potential

Our brains are continuously performing actions that we have no idea are going on. Our brain is constantly doing things like monitoring our immune defence mechanisms, replacing cells, and even working out problems in the back of your subconscious. Your subconscious is a part of your brain working in the background to solve everyday problems and continually guiding you in directions that you may not even be aware of. Have you have ever been stuck on a certain issue and you couldn't see an answer, no matter how hard you concentrated, it just wasn't coming? The part of your brain you are using here is your conscious mind. Then you do something different, for example, you go out to cut the grass in the garden, and something amazing happens. The answer just comes to you. The reason this happens is because the logical conscious part of our brain which is the left side of the brain is very good at reasoning and linear thinking. However, often times it gets stuck in a rut and it isn't creative enough to get you out of it. The right side of the brain, however, is the creative part but, it works the best in the background and not by consciously thinking. So when you let go of concentrating with the left side of the brain, the right brain can then engage with the problem at hand and help you to solve it.

Autosuggestion is a way of influencing your subconscious to start guiding you on a path that you want to follow. This is an example of how your subconscious guides you in a path that you may not even be aware of. If you are starting off in a relationship and deep down inside you do not believe you are anywhere near good enough for the person, you might behave in a way trying to overcompensate for this that smothers your partner and drives them away. If deep down, you thought you were at least equal to their value, you would behave in a more sustainable way.

You may think autosuggestion and the way we talk to our brains is irrelevant or some wishy-washy magic technique. However, there is a lot of scientific evidence backing it up. For example, there is a thing called the placebo effect that has been astonishingly proved over and over again. If a patient thinks they are taking a drug that helps cure their ailment, often times their ailment will be cured regardless of whether the drug was real or just a fake tablet. It even went so far to show that people who thought they underwent knee surgery experienced relief from knee pain despite the surgery never even taking place. The subconscious is powerful and influences everything we do, so it's time to take command of it.

Autosuggestion – The Story of Bill McCall

Bill McCall, who was a popular Australian politician, failed when he established his first business. He suffered the same fate during the first time he ran for a government office. Instead of quitting, he became more motivated. He read different inspirational books to gain the knowledge he needed. He forced his mind to think positively despite everything seeming to be against him. A book called "Think and Grow Rich" taught him this important and effective technique. Using the technique of autosuggestion, he forced himself to fill his mind with creative and positive thoughts.

He wrote his dreams on a piece of paper and read them regularly. He read those statements aloud: with passion and eagerness. With this technique, he felt like he already possessed the things he wanted to have. Consequently, he developed the habits and thoughts processes required by his dreams.

This is an exercise for autosuggestion. Write down your goals on a piece of paper. Read them to yourself every morning and every night before you go to sleep. This alone is not enough to significantly alter your subconscious. To amp this up, you could say these goals thousands of times a day, and this would have a more significant effect. However, there is a more efficient way. Basically, our subconscious will listen to ideas that are repeated over and over again because they must be significant or why would they be repeated so many times, but also it will put importance behind ideas attached to strong emotions. When your subconscious sees that there is an idea with a lot of emotion attached to it, the subconscious will throw this to the front of the cue of importance. So when you read out these ideas, envision them, focus on building your emotional state, your adrenaline levels, feel the excitement of it and envision it so strongly that you are already there, and you can notice what it feels like. If you start doing this type of training for your main goals every day, something powerful starts to happen. Your emotions and subconscious start guiding you to find the ways to achieve these goals. If an opportunity presents itself, your subconscious will home in on it and force you to pay attention to it; it will feel like you are drawn to do so. As if a force of gravity is pulling you.

According to Mr. McCall, the effectiveness of autosuggestion relies on your ability to focus on a particular desire until it becomes a burning passion.

Positive Thinking Exercise - Autosuggestion

Start trying autosuggestion to rewire your brain to get the things you want. Be careful when influencing your subconscious that you are imagining that you do and will have the things you are focussed on. For example a bad thing to say when influencing your subconscious would be: "I need a million dollars," as all this would do would tell your subconscious, because you don't have a million dollars you are not good enough. Focus on imagining things like actually having the million dollars, this way your subconscious will guide you towards it.

Fail Your Way To Victory

Have you experienced failure even after giving all you have?

It's possible that you failed due to your inability to identify and/or utilize something, which is related to your goal. According to Euclid of Alexandria (known as the father of geometry), an object is equal to the totality of its parts but possesses greater value than any of its individual parts. You can link, incorporate, and apply this statement to any output or task you're aiming for.

Negative thinking serves as one of the primary causes of failure. It makes you ignore important powers, facts, and universal laws. Because of negative thinking, you can't apply your skills and knowledge on the activities you need to do. You can't use, influence or control powers that are important to your tasks.

If you are employing positive thinking, you will continue trying. You will strive to find all the "missing pieces." Keep in mind that failure comes to people who, when facing a loss, don't search for the missing pieces.

Things will be extremely easy once you understand the "missing pieces" and gain the requisite knowledge. If you give a complex puzzle to a kid, he may not solve it immediately. If he continues to study the puzzle, he will eventually learn how to put the puzzle pieces together. Then, he can solve it quickly and easily after several more tries.

Thomas Edison is the inventor of the light bulb, the phonograph, and the motion picture camera to name a few. In school, he was told that he was too stupid to learn anything and that he should rely on his good manners to get him through life. Edison Famously failed approximately one thousand times before making the first working light bulb. If Edison had given up even after the first one hundred failures, how different would our world be today? He kept faith and a believed in what he was doing and kept striving for his goal despite an enormous amount of setbacks. There is a phrase used in the science world that there is no such thing as a failed experiment as long as the experiment provides you with new feedback. Edison had to find out what one thousand ways didn't work in order to find one that did.

If you're still in the mindset of "I'm not supposed to fail to achieve success," here are some more famous failures. Michael Jordan was cut from his high school basketball team twice but yet went on to become arguably the greatest basketball player of all time. Oprah Winfrey was fired from her first television reporter job because she was "unfit for TV," She now owns her own network. Albert Einstein couldn't speak until he was four, he was an average student throughout school and failed to get into his first choice university. He then, later on, developed an ability of applying mathematical models to physics and changed modern day science. Walt Disney founder of Disney was fired by the editor of a newspaper because "He lacked imagination." Failure is a stepping stone to success, so anticipate it. Often, failure can be the catalyst, the motivator for success, it can give you strength and drive, just don't give up.

If you have a formula for success, you can make millions of dollars. If you lose money, you have the option to earn it back (or even exceed your previous riches). You just have to determine and apply the formula for success. Succeeding in your first attempt often won't help you discover the formula for your success. You may fail in your next attempt since you didn't learn anything during your first try, it might have just been luck. Adapting to the changes in your environment becomes easy if you know the formula for success and welcome challenges. Through failure, you learn the importance of perseverance and how it is a winner's quality.

Positive Thinking Exercise - Taking a broader view

We never know what events are good and bad in the long run. Something you could perceive as being a bad event, could lead to the greatest achievement in your life. Getting fired could set you on a path to getting your dream job. Try view it in the grander scale, we really don't know what events are good or bad. Try take a broader view of your failures and where they led you.

The Benefits of Having a Problem

Problems will always arise no matter what, if it's plain sailing at the moment you should anticipate a storm. It is, therefore, a benefit to change the way you view problems and flip the script on them. View them as necessary to achieve your best, develop an underlying confidence that no matter what the problem you will survive. Overcoming your problems (especially the hardest ones) helps you improve your skills, knowledge, stature, experience, and self-confidence. After solving a problem, you can expect to become bigger, better, and more successful. If you think about it, all the greatest achievements in the world happened because of a problem that you need to solve. Every problem is an opportunity.

Every person in this world has problems. That's because the universe changes constantly – and people need to work with these changes. Change is a natural law that you can't resist. Your chances of meeting changes successfully depend on the way you view them and deal with them and not by avoiding them.

You have the power to control your thoughts and emotions, thus, you can also control your attitude. You may use, manipulate or influence the changes in your world and within yourself. You can control your destiny. With positive thinking, you can solve all the problems you'll face.

If we are not constantly challenged we become weak, just like if you're in a hospital bed for a long period of time, your muscles waste away, and your bone density decreases, we need to be constantly challenged to keep us strong.

The Story of Charlie Ward

Charlie Ward belonged to a poor family. He started working during his childhood. When he was 34, he was sent to the Leavenworth Penitentiary, because of a crime he didn't commit. He was full of anger during his first few days in the prison. However, it all changed when he decided to be a "positive thinker." He read different books in the prison's library to improve his knowledge about the world. He also did his best to become the best inmate in Leavenworth.

After some time, he became the superintendent of the prison's power plant. Because of his positive thoughts, he was able to turn his life around. When he left prison, he became the company president of a large company called Brown and Bigelow Industries. His management skills were unbelievable: he increased the company's annual sales from $2,000,000+ to $50,000,000+.

If Charlie had never gone to prison, he might never have achieved this level of success. If you want a problem free life, you're in for a shock. The only true way to live a comfortable life is if you learn to get comfortable being uncomfortable, learn to face challenges and develop rock solid confidence that no matter how bad it gets, you will get through it.

The "Do It" Statement

You need to get things done if you want to be successful in life. Having a bright idea is good, but it's usually not enough. You need to turn your idea into something practical and complete the tasks it requires. Here's a basic rule you need to remember: successful people don't leave things half-baked. They do what needs to be done to the best of their abilities.

Starting today, utter the phrase "Do It" whenever you need to do something. Whenever you say this phrase, do the things that you need to do. Never say this phrase if you can't complete the tasks assigned to you. If a task is doable and beneficial, instruct yourself to "Do It" as soon as possible. With regular practice, this statement will be etched onto your subconscious. You will instinctively work on your tasks until you're done.

If you're not used to this kind of "self-starter" statement, practice it with minor tasks. By doing so, you can establish the habit of "acting immediately" during emergency situations or when there is something that you need to do.

Important Note: You need to accomplish your tasks to be a "positive thinker." Positive thoughts will turn sour if you won't act on them and complete the tasks they require. If you fail to act on your ideas, positive thinking can actually have a negative impact on your life.

Positive Thinking Exercise - Positive reframe

The next time something goes wrong, try reframe it in a way that is beneficial to you. For example, if your product launch doesn't go as well as you had hoped. You could say to yourself: "This will cause us to make an even better product, which could sell more than the previous due to its improvements." Spin it in a way that benefits you.

The Most Important Secret Ingredient For All Success

The famous philosopher Confucius once said "He who says he can and he who says he can't are both usually right". Before you achieve anything, you must believe you can, right down to your very core. To achieve any skill or high level of performance, believe that you can do it is an absolute must. This is why; To learn any great skill or accomplish any great act, you must be skilled. Talent is something you are born with; skill is developed through training and practice. All true masters of anything whether it be sport or playing the violin usually have to undergo an apprenticeship of ten thousand hours. This is the number that recurs over and over in people who are at the top of their field. You may be saying well, there are some people who are just born with it. For example, Mozart was a child prodigy, Venus and Serena Williams were outstanding at tennis from a young age. I completely agree they were, but if you follow the breadcrumbs, you see a different story. Mozart's father was a composer and from a ridiculously young age was teaching him the fundamentals of music. Mozart did produce symphonies when he was still very young, but most music critics would agree that these weren't very original, and it was only well after he passed the ten thousand hour mark that he created pieces of true originality and genius. The Williams sisters' father was taking them to tennis courts from when they were very young as well and used to take a garbage can full of tennis balls and make them practice using them. The point is this, you can trace back any real master of their craft back and see the work and skill development that led up to it, you just have to be willing to look.

Don't be disheartened by the ten thousand hour mark and see it as this mountain you have to overcome. This number is involved in people mastering a skill, but you can become extremely competent in many skills a lot faster than this. The point is that you need to put in the effort and the work. Why then would you put in the level of work needed to obtain a high level of competency if you didn't believe you could do it in the first place? You quite simply wouldn't put in the work necessary because it would quite simply be a waste of time. So this is why you need an unflinching belief that you can do it. Only then will you see the payoff and be able to dig down deep and put the work into achieving your goals. Belief is thus the foundation of developing yourself. You must force your mind to believe.

The Story Of Will Smith

Will Smith's father tried to instil the beliefs and positive mental attitudes into Will from a very young age. He raised Will to believe he could do anything. One summer his father tore down a brick wall on the front of his business. Will's father then proceeded to tell the twelve-year-old Will and his brother who was nine to rebuild it. The two kids said that it was "impossible". The job took them a year and a half to complete. His father then told him "Don't you ever tell me there's something you can't do."

Will then went on to become a successful musician and won the first ever Grammy award for best rap performance. Then things took a turn for the worse as one of Will's albums flopped, and by the time he was nineteen, he was broke. Will Smith went from being worth millions to having to drive a motor scooter because it was cheaper on gas. He then moved to Los Angeles. There was a television show called The Arsenio Hall Show. Will simply stood outside the studio nearly every day the show was filming for about a year and a half just meeting people. Then one day he met a man called Benny Medina. Benny is the real life Fresh Prince of Bel-Air. He was going to pitch the idea to the studio when Will met him. The two connected and it was decided that Will was going to be the star of the show. It was a tremendous success and launched Will to stardom once more. Will used the platform of this success as a stepping stone, and then to enter the movie industry. He has taken in nearly 100 million at the box office in almost every movie he stars in. He had lost all his money but due to his mentality and his attitude was not only able to climb back but exceed previous levels of success. You must have an impenetrable belief that you can achieve your goals.

Positivity Exercise - Instil belief

Whatever your goal, you must have unquestioning belief you can do it. Just make up your mind that you are going to do it. You must force yourself to. As without it you'll achieve nothing. Read the books and listen to the motivational speakers that help you to instil this belief. Find what works for you and run with it. What one person can do, another can do.

Conclusion

Thank you again for getting this book.

I hope this book was able to help you master the art of positive thinking and help show you why it is necessary. Remember if you change your mind, you will change your reality.

Finally, if you enjoyed this book, then I'd like to ask you for a favor, would you be kind enough to leave a review for this book on Amazon? It'd be greatly appreciated!

I have also added some bonus material in the following pages. Thank you and good luck!

Preview Of - Conversation: Unlock your personality to be charismatic, charming and memorable with ease

Introduction

Have you ever wondered why you can be funny or charismatic around your friends or family, but suddenly when you try this in other social situations you can't make it to this level or even think of anything fun or interesting to say? This book will teach you that your personality is already good enough; you just need to learn to unleash it and master the art of expressing yourself. This book will teach you:

- How to never run out of things to say

- How to exude confidence when talking to anyone

- How to stand out and be charming and memorable

- How to never feel uncomfortable or out of place in any social setting again

- How to show vulnerability and be loved for it

- How to simply be perceived as cool

- ...and much more

I used to be very introverted, especially with people I didn't know. I studied every book and resource I could get my hands on. After all my research, I finally realized that everyone is charismatic, it's just you have to learn how to unleash it in different situations and environments. Once you know how to access it, it becomes easy, and you feel at home in any social situation.

It's short and to the point, it's not trying to make you a master of gimmicks but actually teach you to show your real personality in a way that people will respect. When you learn to express who you are, you'll unleash a magnetic personality that will help you get the career and relationship success that you've always wanted.

These are some of my other title's on Amazon.

C.A. Barry

<u>Conversation: *Unlock your personality to be charismatic, charming and memorable with ease*</u>

<u>*Happy Life: Reduce Stress And Anxiety, Raise Self Esteem, Have Better Relationships And Be Happy*</u>

<u>*Workout: Sculpt A Hollywood Physique By Using Smart Workout Routines*</u>